JAMAICAN LIKE ME
Written By Sapphire Manley
Illustrated by QBN Studios
AF488078

Paperback ISBN: 979-8-9856492-0-8

Hardcover ISBN: 979-8-9856492-1-5

Ebook ISBN: 979-8-9856492-2-2

This book is dedicated to my grandmother Suzette Wellington-Bajjo, my grandfather Reuben Bajjo and to the rest of my family. Thank you for ensuring I am always well grounded and in connection to my culture and rich heritage.

My mother moved to the
United States when I was
ten months old. She left
everything behind, her
friends, her home, her family.
But she was very excited to
start life over with me.

While living in Jamaica, my mother enjoyed going to the beach, to the local stores and she loved eating tropical fruits. Her favorite fruits were East-Indian mango, sweet-sop and sugar cane. My mother's favorite thing to eat as a child was sugarcanes, oh how she loves the sweet and crunchy taste of a freshly cut sugar cane.

Last summer, I was eight years old when I visited Jamaica for the first time, and I had a wonderful experience, the best time of my life! Jamaica was amazing! I went to visit my cousins in the country area and finally tasted freshly cut sugar cane.

My cousins taught me how to peel the cane with my teeth,
just like my mom said she used to do. It was so refreshing;
I couldn't have imagined how much better it was than
sugar cane in a can that I normally had.

My mother often tells me stories of her childhood, like the summer times she spent visiting her grand-aunt's house and the many trees she and her cousins would climb. They would spend most of their days climbing huge mango, and guinep trees.

I decided to use my
summer days in Jamaica
to do the same. One
day my older cousin and
I decided to see who
could climb the highest
and collect the most
mangoes.

My cousin shouted, "Sapphire I bet you won't be able to climb as high as I can!" and I said "I bet I can climb higher and pick the sweetest mangoes from the top."

"On your mark, get set, GO!"
we both yelled. Then we ran to
the tree and started climbing as
fast as we could. This was my
first time climbing a mango tree.
In fact, this was my first time
climbing any tree at all! I was so
scared that I might fall!

I was trying to climb the tree trunk of this huge monstrous tree, but I kept sliding down. I wondered how I was going to win this race if I can't even get past the trunk. I began to wonder how my mom did this at my age. How did she climb this same tree every day?!

I imagined she was scared at first, just like me. I thought about how her hands and knees were moving very fast, like mine. I imagined that the wind was blowing hard and shaking the leaves and branches, making her scared like it was doing to me.

I don't have mango trees in my city, and I am not allowed to climb the trees in the park. But I do remember rock climbing with my mother and how well I did that, how I got to the top faster than my mother. So, I started to look for parts of the trunk where I could put my feet and hands to pull myself up.

My cousin was now halfway up the tree when she looked down and yelled "Sapphire, are you still coming, I am winning!" I didn't want her to win. I want to prove how well I can climb too! So, I continued to pretend I was rock climbing, I was finally on my way to the top. I was so excited!

My cousin was at the top first and she picked some nice juicy mangoes then she sat on a branch and waited for me to get to the top. I was almost there when I suddenly saw a big green lizard run up my arm. I let out a loud scream and then let go of the branch that I was holding. I was so frightened that I shook the branch and limbs I was standing on.

I had never seen a lizard in person before. I was scared, I couldn't get the lizard off me, it ran into my sleeve, and I could feel it crawling on my body. I started to cry, at this moment I knew I was going to fall because I started jumping around to try and get the lizard out.

My cousin yelled "Sapphire stop, you are shaking the tree and we are going to fall out.!" But I couldn't stop. I wanted that lizard out! She yelled again "Sapphire stop!" I screamed "help me,

I am scared, the lizard is in my shirt!" I was losing my balance and I started to slip off the branch that I was standing on but I could still feel the lizard crawling on my back.

The entire tree was shaking; mangoes began to fall to the ground, and I was about to fall too. I felt the branch shift from under my feet and I tried to hold on with one hand to a small leafy branch.

I was terrified. I then felt my hand sliding down the branch but just when I was about to slide off I felt my cousin grab my hand and pulled me beside her. She said hold on to my arm and relax.

I never felt so relieved in my life!
She then stood beside me and checked
that the lizard was gone and then
showed me how to continue up the tree.
I followed everything she did until we
finally reached the top.

Once at the top she taught me how to
reach for the mangoes and pull them
from the branches. We then sat and ate
mangoes in the tree while we enjoyed
the cool breeze, talked and watched the
people passing below.

On other days, my cousins and new friends taught me how to play some Jamaican games. I loved these games because they were the same games my mother told me she used to play when she was a child.

Outdoor Jamaican games like "dandy shandy" and "bull in-a-pen" were two of my favorites.

To play dandy shandy, we had to walk around the whole yard and search for empty juice boxes and then stuff them with papers and tissues to make the box heavy so we can play. There would be one person at each end with the rest of us in the middle. The aim was to not get hit by the box that was being thrown towards us. The last person standing would win the game. This was my favorite out of them all. It reminded me of dodgeball, except there is someone behind me and in front of me throwing the box.

"Bull-in-a-pen" was my second favorite, we all formed a circle with one person in the middle, we held hands tightly to close the circle. There is one person in the middle of the circle, and they should try their best to try and escape the circle. The middle person who represents a bull should try to run towards our hands and break the circle which represents a bull's pen.

We should hold hands so tightly that the bull cannot escape and wherever the bull is able to escape from, those persons would be eliminated from the game. It was so exciting; we all laughed and squeezed each other's hand so tightly that sometimes I could not feel my fingers.

But I could not lose, I imagined my mother laughing as loudly as I was, enjoying being with cousins just as much as I was.

My mother stayed back
home in Philadelphia
that summer, so I
missed her very much.
But being in Jamaica
and hearing the music
and smelling the food
reminded me so much of
my mother.

She enjoyed listening to different singers. My mother adored both the old and new Jamaican singers from Bob Marley to Koffee. I hear their music everyday as my mother plays them while she is cooking or cleaning the house. I knew some of their songs word for word and was able to sing along while in Jamaica. I felt good because everyone sounded like my mother and sang with the same accent as her.

When my grandma took me out to downtown, Kingston, we would hear music from all singers being played loudly. Some people sang along, and some people went about their day.

Everyone was busy shopping, walking, and talking or eating. I loved the smell, I loved the people, I loved the music and most importantly I loved the food. We could buy all types of juices from many vendors. Orange juice, bag juice, cherry juice, June plum juice and so much more.

My grandmother and I enjoyed stopping at the patty restaurants and having a meal together. I was told many stories when my mom was a child and how she loved to go downtown on some Saturday mornings. My mother loved eating patty from the restaurants too, her favorite was beef patty and chicken patty.

In Philadelphia, there are no restaurants that sells only patty meals but there are frozen patties in the supermarkets and some corner stores. But none taste as delicious as these from the restaurants in Kingston. After shopping in the market, we went to a patty restaurant to relax and eat. Grandma asked, "what type of patty do you want to eat?"
I replied, "since there are only two types, I want both and a soda."

My grandma smiled and said, "when your mother left Jamaica, there weren't many different types of patties, and I know in Philadelphia there is only two main types, but now in Kingston there are a lot more options." I was so elated, finally I get to do something my mother didn't do. Finally, I could tell my mother something new about Jamaica!

I looked up on the menu, then asked "may I please have a lobster patty meal?" My grandma ordered two, one meal for her and one for me. We then sat for a long time just eating, talking and relaxing until it was time to go home.

The time came at the end of Summer when I had to return to Philadelphia so I could prepare for school. I was so sad because I was going to miss my cousins, my grandparents, and my new friends. But I also loved my family and friends in Philadelphia, and I couldn't wait to return to tell them about the awesome summer I had in Jamaica!
I can't wait to return next summer! I can't wait to have more stories to tell my mother! In so many ways I am Jamaican like her and she is Jamaican like me!

About The Author

Sapphire is an eight yr old third grade student who enjoys reading a variety of books and poems from different authors. Sapphire was born in Jamaica but migrated to the USA as a baby where she was raised in Philadelphia with her mother and extended family. She is in love with both countries and enjoys exploring the histories and the beautiful cultures of the USA and Jamaica. Sapphire enjoys connecting with her Jamaican roots and learning about her mother's childhood in Jamaica through learning the games her mother used to play as a child and the food she ate. Every summer is a chance for her to explore her birth culture more as she navigates and embraces the culture of the USA while she is home.

Illustrator Bio

QBN Studios is a small Illustration Studio located in Vernon, Connecticut. Owners Quynh Nguyen and Christopher MacCoy are passionate about helping authors fulfill their, dreams and bring their words to life. QBN Studio's goal is to create an immersive experience for their audiences, to tumble headfirst into imaginary worlds. Follow us on Instagram @qbnstudios for the latest updates on illustrations, books, and other projects.